SORRY
I PEED ♥N YOU

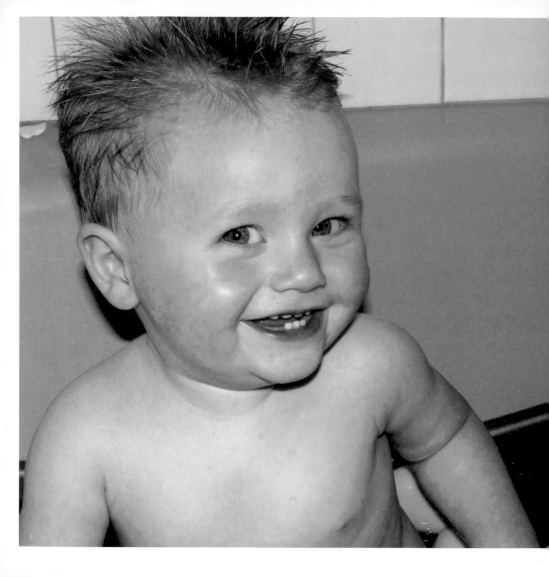

SORRY

♥

(and Other Heartwarming Letters to Mommy)

Jeremy Greenberg

**Andrews McMeel
Publishing, LLC**

Kansas City • Sydney • London

11 12 13 14 15 WKT 10 9 8 7 6 5 4 3 2 1

ISBN: 978-1-4494-0185-6

Library of Congress Control Number: 2010930551

www.sorryipeedonyou.com
www.andrewsmcmeel.com

ATTENTION: SCHOOLS AND BUSINESSES
Andrews McMeel books are available at quantity discounts with bulk purchase for educational, business, or sales promotional use. For information, please write to: Special Sales Department, Andrews McMeel Publishing, LLC, 1130 Walnut Street, Kansas City, Missouri 64106.

For my wonderful sons, Ben and Seth

From: Jack
Age: 27 Months
Re: Enough with the peekaboo

Dear Mommy,

Listen, I don't want to hurt your feelings, and I know that you're just doing it out of fun, but don't you think I'm getting a bit old to be playing peekaboo? Shutting your eyes does not make you invisible. I know you're there. When I was younger, I totally bought it. But I've used the big-boy potty seven times now, and I can point to anything that's yellow. Clearly, my intellect has moved on. Sure, just the other day, you covered your eyes and asked, "Where's Mommy?" to remove your hands only seconds later and say, "Here I am!" and I giggled hysterically. But remember that I paused a second before giggling—it was a polite hint.

There are a lot of new games we can play, Mommy. I'm tall enough to reach the countertops now, so how about "Where's Mommy's Cell Phone?" Or now that I can open the childproof cabinets, we can play "Mommy, Look What I Found in the Garbage."

You're the best mommy in the whole world, and I appreciate your understanding. Please don't get too upset. The last thing anyone wants is a repeat of "I Got Your Nose."

Love,
Jack

Dear Mommy,

There's been a breach in sector 2 of the fish stick containment unit. My fish sticks touched the ketchup and have been rendered inedible. Analysts are trying to figure out how the French fry barrier was breached. Be careful, Mommy. Just to be safe, I'm not going to eat another bite. I know that you're trying to say it's going to be okay, that it's just a little ketchup and that I love ketchup on my French fries. Duly noted, but as a precaution, I think I should evacuate the high chair.

Love,
Kole

From: Kole
Age: 22 Months
Re: Food contamination alert: The fish sticks have touched the ketchup—evacuate the high chair

From: Macy (and Buddy)
Age: 4 Years
Re: Me and my Buddy

Dear Mommy,

Do you think Buddy knows he has four legs? How come Buddy's bed has his name on it, but mine doesn't? I want my name on my bed. If I had four legs could I pee in the yard? Can I pee in the yard if it's my birthday? When is Buddy's birthday? Did Buddy wear diapers when he was a baby? How come Buddy doesn't have any friends? Is Buddy a loser, Mommy?

Buddy and I like to play chase. I chase him, and then he chases me, then I chase him, then he tries to take a nap. I think, "Why is Buddy taking a nap? I've only been chasing him for three hours. Maybe he's hungry." So then I ask you for a snack but throw it on the floor for Buddy. But I think Buddy's still tired. Can you make him a cup of coffee? I gave him a sip of yours while you were in the bathroom, but he just stuck his tongue in it once, sneezed, and went back to sleep—but I think that's because he didn't want to drink your germs.

Love,
Macy

Dear Mommy,

Something's wrong with my jungle gym. It keeps saying "Daddy's out of breath," and "Oh, be careful, honey. Daddy's going to tear his rotator cuff." Why doesn't the jungle gym understand that if it tears its cuff, you'll just hem it like you do your pants? But there's a lot that I love about my jungle gym. The top half can turn bright red when I hang on its neck too long. The jungle gym at the park can't change colors, and the one at the park can't scream, "Ow, honey, that hurts!" either. I am very lucky!

Mommy, I really love my jungle gym, and climbing is very good for my motor skills development. So if the jungle gym *is* running out of breath, can you tell it not to waste any of it complaining about back spasms or slipped discs?

Love,
Madeline

From: Madeline
Age: 17 Months
Re: If Daddy's not a jungle gym, what else could he be?

From: Miles
Age: 16 Months
Re: *Marinara on a Voyage through Space and Time*

Dear Mommy,

You don't seem very happy that I tossed my food against the wall. But please see it not as a wanton act of toddler vandalism. Rather, it is an act of creative expression.

When you're my age, you don't have too many ways to tell the world who you are. I can cry, use the three words I know, or throw food. I call this particular fresco *Marinara on a Voyage through Space and Time*. Many things inspire toddler-food art. I derived my inspiration for this piece from finding a chunk of green bell pepper in the sauce.

One of the things art is supposed to do is create an emotional response in the viewer. Judging by your response, I'd say my creation was a success! Though not all people respond the same. For some reason, my masterpiece made Daddy thirsty, because he stood up and said he needed a drink.

Love,
Miles

Dear Mommy,

Just because I jump higher and giggle louder every time you yell "Sophia, stop jumping on the couch!" it doesn't mean I've got some couch-jumping *problem*. I can stop anytime I want, Mommy. I just jump on the couch to relax, and see what's on the kitchen counters. The fact it makes you and Daddy have faces like you need your diapers changed is an added bonus.

Not only is couch jumping satisfying to *me*, Daddy says if I keep it up, I'll probably satisfy his insurance deductible. So please, Mommy, don't worry. I've been jumping on the couch since I was in diapers—I know what I'm doing.

Love,
Sophia

From: Sophia
Age: 2½ Years
Re: Couch-jumping intervention

From: Elyzabeth
Age: 5 Years
Re: The preschool teacher knows karate. How come you don't know karate?

Dear Mommy,

Today Ms. Jenny, the preschool teacher, brought her special hairless cat to class, and we all got to pet it. Ms. Jenny sneezes at other types of cats, and I think I do, too. If we got a cat, I'd want one just like Ms. Jenny's, and she could come over and bring her cat, and the cats could play together.

And you should hear how Ms. Jenny reads books, Mommy. She has the most beautiful voice. Not that you don't. But it's like she sings the words. She says she learned to sing from the birds in her yard when she's gardening. Ms. Jenny can talk to birds, Mommy, and they land on her fingers as she sings and walks through her garden.

Ms. Jenny says that everyone should care about the environment, and that's why she rides her bicycle to work. Why don't you ride your bike to work? How come you don't garden? Why can't you talk to birds? Can we get a cat?

But even though Ms. Jenny is super-amazing, she isn't there for me when I have the sniffles or when I'm hungry, so I still love you more.

Love,
Elyzabeth

Dear Mommy,

You know how you keep telling me "You don't have to yell"? I know I don't have to, Mommy. I *want* to.

Sometimes I think that you don't like it when I yell, even if I'm piercing your eardrums with the words you're so happy I'm learning, such as "No!" and "More!" and not just shrieks and shouts. But then I think, "How could that be?" I love to yell, so why wouldn't you love to hear me yell?

I think you should just relax and learn to enjoy my long, shrill, high-pitched shrieks. I won't have impulse control until I'm at least three years old. You know how Daddy can't stop saying those bad words when his favorite team is on TV? That's how I'll be until I start preschool.

Love,
Arabella

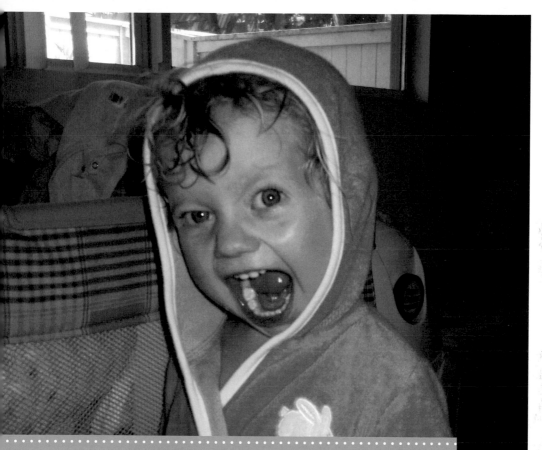

From: Arabella
Age: 23 Months
Re: But if I'm indoors, then this must be my indoor voice

From: Ben
Age: 21 Months
Re: It's too hot for pajamas

Dear Mommy,

I don't know if you noticed, but Daddy's been wearing shorts for at least a month now, and during the day you can hear the bigger kids swimming in a nearby pool. It's summertime, Mommy; please don't bundle me for bed as though we live in an igloo.

I know that I'm small, so you can't tell how warm I am. But I was hoping the pools of sweat in my footsies might be a clue. When I started squirming as you were putting me into my PJs last night, it wasn't because I wanted to stay up later. I didn't want to be cocooned in my winter sleeper after a day when you could fry an egg on the sidewalk.

Why don't you just let me sleep in my diaper but put some blankies in the crib; I can grab them if I get cold. Now you can feel like you're doing your best to keep me from getting sick, and I can stop having weird dreams about being in a sauna with Elmo.

Love,
Ben

Dear Mommy,

Yesterday, Daddy said *shit*. He told me not to tell you that he said *shit* in front of me, because he said that you'd be upset, because then I'd copy him and start using *shit* when I talk. But I told him he didn't have to worry, because I know *shit* is a bad word. I'm only using *shit* right now so I can tell you that Daddy said *shit*—right after he accidentally backed over the trash cans.

Please don't be too mad at Daddy. He doesn't know why this *shit* always happens to him. He just knows that *shit* happens. Then Daddy's boss called him as he was picking up the garbage. Mommy, why does *shit* roll downhill? Does *shit* have to wear a helmet like I do when I ride my bike down our hill? Who is rolling *shit* downhill? Judging by the look on your face, I'd say that you don't know about half the *shit* I'm talking about. That's okay. I guess that's just the way *shit* is sometimes.

Love,
Ethan

From: Ethan
Age: 4 Years
Re: Daddy said *shit*

From: Seth
Age: 7 Months
Re: Sorry I peed on you

Dear Mommy,

First of all, let me tell you that I was just as surprised as you were. No baby ever wakes up one morning and thinks "Today is the day I'm going to pee on my mommy." Someone must've left a window open, because that breeze hit just as the diaper came off, and before I knew it, I'd entered you in a wet T-shirt contest. I'm too young to know what embarrassment is, but as someone who pees on himself all day long, I can tell you that I know what it's like, and it's not pleasant.

I won't be able to control my pee muscle for at least another year, and probably longer. Remember how when I was a newborn you'd keep a towel handy in case I sprung a leak? You may want to start doing that again. It will greatly reduce the chances of my first words being "Crap! This was my last clean shirt!"

I'm truly sorry, Mommy, and will try not to pee on you ever again unless I have a very good reason.

Love,
Seth

Dear Mommy,

Remember yesterday when we accidentally got off the freeway in the part of the city where Daddy always says to lock the doors? And on that wall was an amazing mural? It had all kinds of names, and I think I saw what looked like a hand with one finger? Well, when I saw that, I thought, "Why can't our toilet be as colorful as an inner-city freeway underpass?" So earlier today when you became distracted by answering the phone, *voilà!*

I have lived in this house for three years now, Mommy, and I thought it'd be nice to draw something that tells the world a toddler is part of this community and that she's committed to transforming her environment.

I suppose if you don't want me to represent my toddler culture, you can use a blow dryer to melt off the crayon. I just thought it'd be nice to make my mark.

Love,
Louise

From: Louise
Age: 3 Years
Re: The bathroom beautification initiative

From: Gage
Age: 22 Months
Re: Look how far I can throw my sippy cup

Dear Mommy,

I have something amazing to show you! Look at how far I can throw my sippy cup! I can throw it from my high chair clear across the kitchen table. And if I aim perfectly, I can knock over any water glasses and ketchup bottles. And that's with the sippy cup half full. Can you imagine the distance I'd get if I actually drank all my milk?

But I wonder why you and Daddy never throw *your* cups. I'm guessing the reason is that you just haven't had a knowledgeable toddler explain how to do it. There are two perfect times to hurl your sippy cup. First is when people are least expecting it. Just right in the middle of a meal, pick it up and throw it on the floor, toward the dog's head, or across the table. Second is if someone asks, "Do you need more milk?" you can answer the question with a simple chuck of the sippy cup.

With a little practice, Mommy, you'll be able to throw your sippy cup so hard against the floor that you'll be able to dent the hardwoods just like I can.

Love,
Gage

Dear Mommy,

There's something I've been meaning to ask you, and now that we're in a busy supermarket full of strangers, I think it's finally the right moment. Mommy, what's a vagina? Last time I asked, you said, "Honey, ask me about that later," as everyone stared at us in the doctor's office. I'd still really like to know.

Apparently, a lot of people want to know what a vagina is, Mommy, because everyone's looking at us, and a few are laughing. So, is this a good place to tell me what a vagina is? Do I have a vagina? Does Daddy have a vagina? What about Princess the cat? Do they sell vaginas at this store? Everyone keeps staring, so maybe we all need to know. Would you tell the entire store what a vagina is, Mommy?

Love,
Zach

From: Zach
Age: 3 Years
Re: Is this crowded supermarket the right place to ask what a vagina is?

From: Wyatt
Age: 2½ Years
Re: Preschool gives me a tummy ache

Dear Mommy,

Thank you for picking me up early from preschool. Something about that place was giving me a tummy ache. I don't know what. All I had to eat today was my normal food that you packed me, plus two crayons, three ounces of Elmer's glue, a piece of construction paper, three boogers, and an ounce of glitter. What do you think it could be? And what's a culinary academy? The teacher says that's what I've confused her class for.

Anyway, it's great to see you. Why are you all sweaty and wearing a jog bra and running shoes? Were you doing something?

Love,
Wyatt

Dear Mommy,

Why do I cry *every* time you leave me at the YMCA day care? Well, have you asked yourself how you'd feel if I *didn't* cry, and played nicely as though you weren't the center of my universe? The fact that you haven't been able to get a workout in since I was born is a sign of love, Mommy.

I know you still want to exercise, so I have created the "never leave my sight" workout just for you! Every day, I'll make sure you do at least ten pick-me-up-for-no-reasons, three clean-up-the-blocks-after-I-scatter-them-needlessly-about-the-house, and twenty-five ah-ah-ahhhs! which involve seeing me about to toss my food on the floor, so you run as fast as you can over to the high chair yelling, "Ah-ah-ahhh, don't!"

One day when I'm a teenager, I'll cry if I *can't* leave your sight. You should appreciate the barnacle years.

Love,
Alexis

From: Alexis

Age: 15 Months

Re: I'm sorry I cried, but you were gone for five minutes. What was I supposed to do?

From: Max
Age: 18 Months
Re: Please let me go down the slide by myself

Dear Mommy,

Okay, maybe running away from you at the park yesterday was a bit childish. And I do regret tossing my shoe in the trash. I honestly didn't know someone had just thrown out day-old potato salad. But what else could I do? I'm almost 20 months old, and you still won't let me go down the slide by myself! It's embarrassing, Mommy. That little toddler girl in pink-bowed pigtails didn't even look at me once while we were at the park—and that's even after I'd demonstrated supreme agility by running across the bouncy bridge. How am I ever going to get bitten or chased by a girl if she thinks I still need to slide with my mommy?

I'm ready to go down both the straight and curly slides by myself. But we can just start with the straight slide. And you can even wait at the bottom of the slide and say "Come to Mommy." You don't have to. But I know this might be a tough transition for you, so I'm willing to let you take baby steps.

Love,
Max

Dear Mommy,

I am so excited that you're taking me to play in the yard! I will try to stay out of the garden and will be respectful of which balls belong to the dog and which are mine. I also have some great news! I no longer have to wear shoes while playing in the backyard. Yesterday, while you were out shopping, Daddy took me outside to play. He was about to put my jacket on but couldn't find it, so he said, "It's pretty warm out." Then he asked, "Brooke, honey, where are your shoes?" He looked for about two seconds and then was like, "Forget it. It's just grass."

That's why I'm wormy-squirming as you try to cram my feet into shoes. I just prefer to be barefoot—like Daddy lets me. Also, Daddy lets me eat while standing up in the kitchen. I like that, too. Next time Nana comes over, can we all eat standing in the kitchen?

Love,
Brooke

From: Brooke
Age: 2 Years
Re: But *Daddy* doesn't make me wear shoes

From: Olivine
Age: 10 Months
Re: Dirt: It's what's for dinner

Dear Mommy,

You know how you're always asking me to try new foods? I would like to return the favor and offer you a handful of a local backyard delicacy I call *dirt*.

Dirt, or mud as it's known when it's wet, is very healthy, and it's full of minerals—plus the occasional rock or worm. For your first serving, I recommend something from the vegetable garden, because it's soft, and you can grab and swallow a handful before anyone yells "Oh my God, that's gross—your baby just ate dirt!"

I don't want you to worry about getting sick from the dirt. In fact, scientists believe eating dirt is actually an instinctual way to introduce bacteria that strengthen the immune system. And for all the colds I'll be bringing home from preschool, Mommy, you're gonna need all the dirt you can get.

Love,
Olivine

Dear Mommy,

Why is it that you won't let the dog lick my face clean of the frosting, but when you can't find a washcloth, you'll lick your hand and wash me like a cat? Personally, I think I look very cute covered in cupcake. And it's not that I have anything against your saliva. As mommies go, I'm sure you've got some of the best saliva around. I'm sure your spit is the envy of your moms' club, and Windex keeps calling to see if they can tap your salivary glands and make the first-ever bottled toddler-face cleaner.

But I'm a kid. You should be happy that your yummy homemade frosting is the *only* thing I have on my face. I know that you can't let me walk around wearing food. But your cupcakes are just too yummy. If you didn't want my face covered in frosting, you should've had Aunt Lauren make them. It would be completely clean.

Love,
Jocelyn

From: Jocelyn
Age: 2½ Years
Re: Mommy, your saliva is not a soap substitute

From: Wyatt
Age: 9 Months
Re: Doggy trapped inside a boy's body

Dear Mommy,

Guess what? Today I am a doggy! I have to warn you that I will be licking you, Daddy, my older sister, and the other doggy. You may find this gross, but it's just what we dogs do. If you say "no" and "off" in human words, I will only respond in Bark—the language of my species.

The only time I won't be a doggy is when you tell me that doggies can't have ice cream. There's a special provision in my dogginess that allows me to go back to being a toddler when ice cream is involved. When I'm done, I'll wag my hand as though it were my tail, to show I have a happy belly.

Mommy, thank you for accepting me as a doggy. There's nothing you could've done to prevent this transformation. I just have a very good imagination, and I'll probably grow out of it as soon as I learn that doggies don't get birthday presents.

Love,
Wyatt

Dear Mommy,

I know that after a long day of chasing me around the house, you were probably happy that all you had left was to give me a quick bath and then off to bed. But as you can see by what just surfaced, there's been a change in plans. The tub just became a potty.

Please don't blame yourself. Some mommies might worry that they bathed their kid too soon after dinner, or that maybe the baby's got a sore butt, so the warm water helps them poop. My butt is fine, and you did wait long enough after dinner. I just wasn't completely done pooping when you changed my diaper. I was going to mention it, but you seemed so tired, I didn't want to make a big stink about it. But I gotta tell ya, Mommy, there's nothing like a poop in the bathtub after a long day.

While it is yucky, there's nothing to worry about. Even if I drink a little poop water, I should be okay, because my body is already familiar with the bacteria. But you will have to drain, wash, and refill the tub. And this time, because it's late, I'll only pee in it.

Love,
Roman

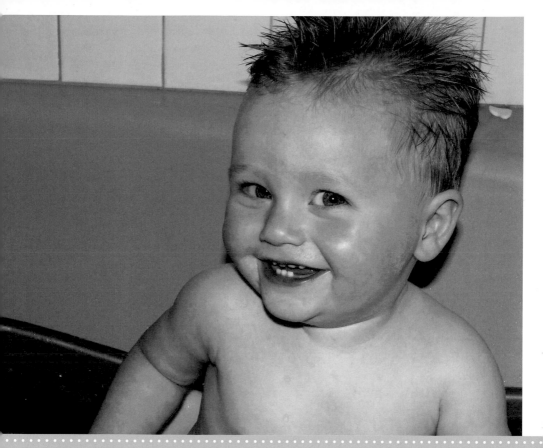

From: Roman
Age: 15 Months
Re: All I'm saying is drain the tub and don't reach for the soap

From: Sydney

Age: 20 Months

Re: If you don't let me stay outside, life as we know it will come to an end

Dear Mommy,

I am *not* ready to go back in the house! I see you trying to ignore me and acting all calm and patient. But just wait; all I've done so far is *scream* at the top of my lungs. That's a stage 1 tantrum. If you keep pretending the world isn't coming to an end, I'll take my tantrum up to stage 2: foot stomping *and* screaming. If you say, "But Sydney, dear, it's time for dinner," you'd better find a bench to crawl under, because you'll then be caught in the eye of a stage 3 tantrum, which involves collapsing on the ground, kicking and punching dirt, and my patented *scryming*—a unique blend of screaming and crying. Stage 3 tantrums are very rare, but since I missed my nap and wouldn't eat my lunch, the chances for a catastrophic toddler event are very high.

Your only hope of averting disaster is to let me stay outside. Even then, I'm really tired, so I might explode anyway. Actually, do we have any cookies? I'm kind of hungry, Mommy. I want to go inside and have a cookie.

Love,
Sydney

Dear Mommy,

Remember how I had a cold three days ago, and I couldn't go to day care, and you had to stay home from your job as a parma-cutical rep? Well, now that you're sick, and you have to stay home because people don't buy from boogery parma-cutical reps, I am going to take care of you as good as you took care of me.

When we get home, you can just lie in bed, and I'll make you lunch. I hope you like ice cream covered in frozen peas. I'd make you something else, but I can only reach the freezer. I'm sure if I mix those things up, it'll be yummy.

I just want you to know that I'm sorry I got you sick, and I promise it will only happen 327 more times before I start elementary school.

Love,
Madeline

From: Madeline
Age: 2 Years
Re: Oh, my gosh! Did I get you sick?

From: Billy
Age: 22 Months
Re: These aren't "Shrek ears"!

Dear Mommy,

Wait a second. This is broccoli, isn't it? You said they were Shrek ears and that they were yummy. But I remember this stuff from last week, when you said they were called Incredible Hulk noses, and tried serving them buried in a river of cheddar cheese. I even took a bite. But then Daddy walked in the room and said, "Look at that. He's eating broccoli." I'm eating *what*? Broccoli does not sound like something a toddler should be eating! Then, after you yelled at Daddy, and I wouldn't eat the broccoli, you ate a piece yourself and made those "nom nom nom" yummy sounds. I love you for the effort, Mommy. But face facts: Broccoli is the yuckiest substance known to kids.

Please don't take this personally, Mommy. In a way, I'm actually doing you a favor. You're always saying broccoli's so high in fiber. But I am still in diapers. Do you really want to add more fiber to my diet?

As I get older, my taste buds will change, and I may grow to love broccoli. But until then, anytime you feel inspired to make me eat something green, try a bowl of mint chip ice cream.

Love,
Billy

Dear Mommy,

You're probably wondering why I was about to climb into the refrigerator. Well, before I get into that, I want you to notice that I don't have my shoes on. That's because I know you have a strict "no wearing shoes while standing in the refrigerator" rule, and I respect that.

And I don't have my socks on, either. I know you put socks on me because you said it's getting cold in the house, and I could get sick. But then I thought about my poor milk. It doesn't have any socks, and it's probably very cold in the refrigerator. How can I wear socks when my poor milk is freezing? So I opened the door to let it warm up. That way the milk won't get sick, Mommy. And since I was already in the fridge, I figured I'd have some salami.

I also tossed the jalapeño dip on the floor, because you told me jalapeños are hot. Since the doggy doesn't have any socks, either, he can eat the jalapeños and be so warm and toasty that he'll probably ask to go outside all night long.

Love,
John

From: John
Age: 23 Months
Re: What shelf did you say it was on?

From: Atticus
Age: 23 Months
Re: Had it with my hat

Dear Mommy,

I understand that I've got amazing, baby-soft skin. But if the price of this skin is wearing *this* hat, I'd rather look like Nana's neck. And the hat's so itchy, Mommy. Was it made from poison oak? Why does it say "Lifeguard"? I haven't even taken swimming lessons. Do you have to get *all* my clothes from garage sales? Daddy's hats are awesome and say things like "I'm with Stupid" or "Free Breast Exams." Can I also offer free breast exams or be with stupid?

But even if you got me a cool hat, I probably wouldn't wear that one, either. I just don't want anything on my head unless it's not supposed to be there. If you really wish to cover me up, send me outside wearing a laundry basket or training potty. And half the reason I don't want to wear my hat is because it's *my* hat. If you said, "Atticus, you cannot wear this hat! It's Mommy's," well, I'd wear that hat all day long, and there'd be nothing you could do to stop me.

Love,
Atticus

Dear Mommy,

I am so happy you're here to witness this proud day in baby history! I have just become the first toddler to make the solo climb to the top of Mount Kitchen Table. It wasn't easy. Several previous tries were aborted when you'd run up and yank me off of the chair that leads to the summit. You even went so far as to remove all the chairs from the table, forcing me to remain at base camp for weeks. But then you put the chairs back and were momentarily distracted by a phone call. That's when I knew conditions were perfect to reach the top.

I know that many toddlers have tried to reach the summit of Mount Kitchen Table. Even the cat, on several occasions, has briefly reached the peak, only to have you yell "Get that cat off the table!" And to answer your question "Why do you keep trying to climb onto the table?" Because it is there, Mommy. Because it is there.

Love,
Annie

From: Annie
Age: 2½ Years
Re: The first toddler to the top of Mount Kitchen Table

From: Arden
Age: 3½ Months
Re: I'm guessing you weren't allowed to have dolls as a child

Dear Mommy,

I'm glad sticking stuff on my head amuses you. I know that I still wake you up at night with my crying, so if dressing me like this helps remind you how cute I am and relieves some stress, I'm happy. And I must admit that I do look very cute. It's not every infant who can pull off the green-stripes-with-a-single-pink-polka-dot-pacifier-clip look. But this thing you stuck on my head makes me wonder if you have an unfulfilled fantasy of being a Vegas showgirl.

You've got about six more months of putting stuff on my head before I start to become aware of how important clothes are. I will then drive you crazy getting dressed every morning. You'll wish you'd dressed me in a potato sack, and it'll be a good thing that you've got the little shopping cart. Because if I don't like my outfit, it'll be the only way you'll get me outside.

Love,
Arden

ACKNOWLEDGMENTS

I would first like to thank this book's wonderful editor and an incredibly awesome person, Lane Butler, to whom I am profoundly grateful for her unending faith in my projects. Huge thanks also to my excellent agent, David Fugate, for his subtle wisdom; and to the very gifted Nicole Ghazal at MSN, for bringing in a fresh voice and allowing me to share my life with millions of parents. I, of course, still bow to the guru, Chris Federico.

I would also like to thank Kathy Hilliard for her great promotional work; everyone else at Andrews McMeel for working their butts off to make this book great; and all the people at team MSN who graciously made room for The Family Room.

Very special thanks as well to Jessica Smith, Ginger Young Fisher, Ashley Cochran, Monika Orrey, and Sam Thorpe—for taking time from their busy lives to help that crazy kid from school.

This book wouldn't exist without all of the wonderful families who contributed their photos. Thank you to the Chengs, the Cochrans, the Doyles, the Fischers, the Frenches, the Fugates, the Galantes, the Ghazals, the Greenbergs, the Grossmans, the Heffners, the Logelins, the Neises, the Romyns, the Smiths, the Tiches, the Wards, and the Young Fishers.

Also, huge thanks to all of the excellent photographers who allowed their work to appear in the book: Sara Benson, "Wyatt's First Day of Preschool," page 34; Kyle Connolly, "Concerned Kid," page 53; Abra Cook, "Yummy Dirt," page 42; Greg Dodson, "Shoeless in December," page 41; Amanda Hatton, "Grumpy at the Barn," page 50; Jorge Moreno Jr., "Couch Jumping," page 17; Roland Polczer, "Kid in the Market," page 33; and Laura Yurs, "Toddler Graffiti" page 29.

Let me save my absolute deepest thanks for my family: First and foremost to my wonderful wife, Barbara, for putting up with my long hours and for believing; to my sons, Ben and Seth, for being funnier than me; and to my parents and Arlene, Lauren, Jonathan, Ryann, Ethan, Ava, and Dagny; and to everyone else I have known and been inspired by. Thank you!